IMAGES
of America

HISTORIC SEARS, ROEBUCK AND CO. CATALOG PLANT

THE SEARS CATALOG PLANT
1906 and Today

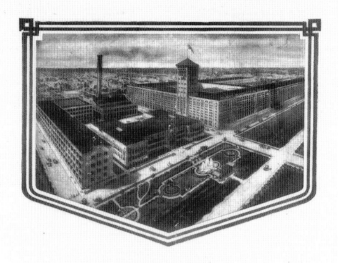

SEARS CATALOG PLANT, 1906, AND HOMAN SQUARE, 2003. This image presents a side-by-side comparison of the main grounds covering nearly a century. The complex is surprisingly intact with the exception of new housing to the east, the Allstate Building to the south, and the replacement of the Merchandise Building distribution facilities with the state-of-the-art Homan Square Community Center to the north. (Courtesy of the Real Estate Capital Institute.)

IMAGES
of America

HISTORIC SEARS, ROEBUCK AND CO. CATALOG PLANT

John M. Oharenko with the
Homan Arthington Foundation

Published by Arcadia Publishing
Charleston SC, Chicago IL, Portsmouth NH, San Francisco CA

Printed in Great Britain

Library of Congress Catalog Card Number: 2005929344

For all general information contact Arcadia Publishing at:
Telephone 843-853-2070
Fax 843-853-0044
E-mail sales@arcadiapublishing.com
For customer service and orders:
Toll-Free 1-888-313-2665

Visit us on the Internet at http://www.arcadiapublishing.com

For more information about the Catalog Plant, please visit http://www.originaltower.com.

SEARS CATALOG PLANT 100TH ANNIVERSARY LOGO. This seal features the original Sears Tower and the administrative building.

CONTENTS

Acknowledgments   6

Introduction   7

1.   Great Idea   11

2.   Great Buildings   39

3.   Great Artifacts   103

4.   Great People   111

5.   Great Location   117

ACKNOWLEDGMENTS

I am very grateful to Charlie Shaw, Kristin Dean, and Laura Lode of the Homan Arthington Foundation for introducing me to the hidden treasures of the original Sears, Roebuck and Co. and the North Lawndale community. The foundation helped in the collection of a variety of pictures, documents, and verbal communications about some of the great triumphs associated with this area.

I am also indebted to a variety of other individuals, organizations, and institutions with roots on the West Side, as well as with Sears, Roebuck and Co., Homan Square, and Sterling Park. A partial list of people contributing information to this book includes the following: Andy Chychula, Anne Garza, Myron Lyskanycz, Scott Maesel, and Mark Ross. The Sears Archives staff, the Chicago Historical Society research staff, the Chicago Planning Department, and WLS Radio were very patient and helpful in processing my countless inquiries for data and photographs about the complex.

Last, but not least, my parents—Vladimir and Lubomyra Oharenko—sparked in me a love for the city of Chicago, of which I have been a lifelong resident since growing up in the West Side Ukrainian Village, only three miles from the plant. My parents have given me boundless energy and encouragement throughout my life.

CHARLES F. MORAN (1936–2003). This book is dedicated to Charley Moran, a Sears senior executive for 40 years and the president of the Homan Arthington Foundation. Unfortunately, he passed away in 2003 during this book's writing. His spirit and energy have guided us all.

INTRODUCTION

*Nothing more clearly dramatized the metamorphosis of Sears Roebuck from a
promotional circus to a great institution than the new building complex.
The newspaper and magazine writers were exhilarated by a tour. Sears Roebuck seemed
the very symbol of the new technology and efficiency of the new century.
It seemed a colossus of distribution. It became the pride of Chicago.*
—Cecil Hoge Sr., *The First Hundred Years are the Toughest*, 1988

The story of Sears, Roebuck and Co. spans more than a century and reinforces the foundations of modern life in the United States. Sears is truly one of America's great retail icons, and much of its fame and fortune is tied to the original catalog plant built on Chicago's West Side in 1906. The facility served as the company's world headquarters until the firm moved into the current Sears Tower—the tallest building in North America—in 1973.

When Richard Sears and Julius Rosenwald began construction on their West Side Chicago headquarters in the early 1900s, they could never have realized the lasting impact they would make on 100 years of neighborhood history. The North Lawndale community, surrounding the intersection of Homan Avenue and Arthington Street, became home to one of the world's great retailing empires.

The facilities constructed to support the growth of this enterprise were both a crowning achievement and physical proof of a world-class organization. The Sears complex was a bold statement of commerce, demonstrating the harmony of raw efficiency with architecture. The facility handled all the demands of the largest scale of retailing including printing catalogs, managing client relations, processing orders, some manufacturing, strategic planning, and research.

Spanning nearly seven decades of service, the plant was home to many great ideas and concepts including, but not limited to, the following: the original Sears Tower and Catalog Printing Facilities (1906), one of the first corporate profit-sharing programs (1916), WLS Radio (1924), Sears's first retail outlet (1926), Allstate Insurance (1931), and the Homart Development Company (1959). And thanks to Sears's commitment to Chicago and North Lawndale, the complex was not abandoned after the company moved.

Today, much of the complex exists as proof of the company's ingenuity, creativity—and ultimately—its success. The North Lawndale neighborhood is taking advantage of the old Sears district for its own purposes. Under the new name of Homan Square, many of the same principles of greatness and harmony are shaping a renewed community, which is making its own national impact. The complex continues as a thriving focal point of Chicago's West Side and includes many of the original structures, along with over 300 homes and a state-of-the-art community center.

This volume will highlight the accomplishments of Sears, Roebuck and Co. at its original West Side Chicago headquarters. It will also tell the developing story of Homan Square and its creative reuse of physical structures.

The team of founder Richard Sears and president Julius Rosenwald proved an ideal blend of talents for creating remarkable commercial success. Sears was an entrepreneurial promoter with an uncanny knack for writing advertising copy that appealed to rural Americans. He lacked an understanding of effective distribution and organizational management, however. Julius Rosenwald, with a strong moral character, understood how to blend labor and materials within a highly efficient corporate environment. He combined Sears's promotional flair with a money-back guarantee.

This entrepreneurial pairing created a 13-fold growth of the fledgling mail-order business during the final five years of the 19th century. Sales grew from $750,000 a year in 1895 to $10 million in 1900. The organization therefore needed to build a distribution and operations facility that could handle such staggering growth and deliver on the promise of complete customer satisfaction. In other words, Sears needed buildings literally constructed on a foundation of trust.

The company hired the finest architects, planners, builders, and craftsman. Every effort was made to visually blend the commercial structures to the surrounding parks and boulevards, and the new and residential district of North Lawndale. Architects Nimmons and Fellows had just finished refining Italianate Renaissance architecture (San Minato in Florence, Tuscany) with the practical principles of the Chicago School. Construction began in earnest in 1905. The scale of work is astonishing even by today's standards. Some 7,000 artisans and laborers were working on the building at one time. And 353,000 bricks were laid within eight hours.

According to builder Theodore Starrett in an article in the April 1906 edition of the *Architectural Record*, in one instance, workers nearly ran out of materials, then immediately confiscated a train engine and ran without orders 15 miles to the transfer point, where the cars of brick were waiting. On another occasion, a flat car ran off the track where a wall was to be constructed. The person in charge said to brick in the railcar to avoid construction delays; however, a wrecking crew was able to salvage the car before construction continued.

The result was a three-million-square-foot state-of-the-art catalog facility that maximized the benefits of shipping by rail. A description in the 1906 Sears catalog stated, "Miles of railroad tracks run through, in and around this building for the receiving, moving and forwarding of merchandise; elevators, mechanical conveyors, endless chains, moving sidewalks, gravity chutes, apparatus and conveyors, pneumatic tubes and every known mechanical appliance for reducing labor, for the working out of economy and dispatch is to be utilized here in our great Works."

One upshot of this massive construction effort was a severe reduction to the company's working capital balances. Rosenwald tapped Henry Sachs of Goldman Sachs for $5 million to repay bank loans. Questioning the adequacy of $5 million, Goldman Sachs partnered with investment firm Lehman Brothers to raise $40 million in a combination issue of $10 million in preferred stock and $30 million in common stock.

With sufficient working capital and a strong managerial force, Sears continued to grow from the 1900 sales of $10 million to $50 million in 1907 and on to $235 million in 1920.

Sears, Roebuck and Co. needed a final talent to fill an emerging gap in the operation of a new state-of-the-art mail order complex. Otto Doering joined the organization to orchestrate masterful operating systems for order taking and product delivery in the shortest time possible with the least amount of errors—an important ingredient in the recipe for total customer satisfaction.

Upon completion of the facilities in 1906 and under the management of these three bright stars, Sears, Roebuck and Co. grew 23-fold during the next 20 years and remained the largest catalog house in the world.

At the end of World War I, a sea of technological and lifestyle changes swept the country, changing the face of the Catalog Era. WLS ("World's Largest Store") Radio began broadcasting with Gene Autrey from the original Sears Tower at Homan Avenue and Arthington Street, Charles Lindbergh showed the potential of modern aviation, and most of all, Americans fell in love with their cars. The automobile not only revolutionized transportation, but began to define the shape of cities and the American economy. Catalogs targeting rural farm families were no longer the most important marketing tool. Customers with cars could drive to retail facilities and actually see and touch the goods.

When he joined Sears in 1924, Gen. Robert Wood already understood the shifting behavior of customers. He had been an executive at rival Montgomery Ward and foresaw how the popularity of automobiles would bring more rural customers to urban stores. In 1925, Sears opened its first retail store in Chicago at Homan Avenue and Arthington Street. By the end of the decade, Sears had more than 300 stores and Wood had become president of the company

The "Great Store" vision catapulted Sears, Roebuck and Co. from a mail-order catalog firm to the nation's biggest retail chain. Selling everything from washing machines to televisions and baseball gloves under one roof was good business. Even the Great Depression could not stop the expansion. In 1931, Sears's retail store sales surpassed that of its mail-order business; that same year, Wood entered the world of automobile insurance by creating Allstate Insurance Company. Sears became the first retail chain to set aside free parking areas next to its stores.

When World War II ended, Sears ranked only slightly ahead of Montgomery Ward. When Wood retired in 1954, Sears's $3 billion in sales was triple that of its rival. A little more than a decade later, Sears became the largest retailer in the world and the first to hit $1 billion in monthly sales. The phenomenal growth would eventually lead to the unthinkable: Sears was now too small for its colossal West Side headquarters.

Sears continued to expand during the 1960s and 1970s. However, the company's success meant that its days at Homan Avenue and Arthington Street were numbered. Yet, Sears remained committed to the area. The company eventually relocated to the new Sears Tower downtown in 1973, while still maintaining the West Side facilities as additional warehousing and distribution outlets for over another decade.

In 1988, chairman Ed Brennan reached a major crossroads involving the company and the West Side facilities. As a responsible business and civic leader, Brennan wanted to save the complex and help the North Lawndale community. He knew the legacy firsthand and remained true to his roots. (As a child he had visited Santa Claus at the Homan and Arthington store.)

Ed Brennan needed to find a partner who could preserve the legacy of the then 80-year-old property while addressing the contemporary needs of the area. He reached out to Charles H. Shaw, a Chicago developer with a reputation for crafting innovative approaches to challenging large real estate projects. Shaw already knew the West Side and was clearly the person who could get the job done.

After nearly a year of exploratory meetings with community and city leaders including Mayor Daley, Shaw brought Sears a recommendation. He proposed a long-range, three-pronged approach. The redeveloped property would be named Homan Square and would address significant community needs for housing, social services, and economic development.

Ed Brennan and Sears liked the idea and joined the city of Chicago in pledging millions in financial support and infrastructure improvements. Shaw set to work capturing the rental potential of the headquarters building at 3333 West Arthington and began laying plans for low-rise, mixed-income housing. Charles F. Moran, a former Sears senior vice-president who had once headed the catalog facility, signed on as an invaluable voluntary advisor. The slogan "New Life for North Lawndale" was coined to describe the effort.

As a group of non-profits and small business began moving into offices at 3333 West Arlington, the first phase of single-family homes started rising across the street. Some 15 years and hundreds of millions of dollars in investment later, the community had a new anchor. More than 300 new units of affordable, for-sale and rental housing were built and occupied. The 3333 West Arlington building was now home to a diverse mix of local entrepreneurs and community service organizations, including the district office of a United States congressman. The creation of a mixed-income housing market encouraged commercial developers, who constructed a new retail shopping center with a grocery store and cineplex blocks away on Roosevelt Road.

One

GREAT IDEA

The entire Pullman City—the talk of the civilized world ten years earlier—could fit into the Merchandise Building; The [plant's] mail volume exceeds that of the City of Milwaukee.
—Plant builder Theodore Starrett, *Architectural Record*, April 1906

The original Sears catalog complex, now known as Homan Square, was once again exhibiting the principles of greatness and harmony that had characterized its origins. One troubling remnant of the past remained stubbornly intact, however: the dire economic and social conditions of residents surrounding the square.

In December 2001, Mayor Richard M. Daley cut the ribbon officially opening the $28 million Homan Square Community Center. The brand-new 70,000-square-foot center is currently home to a group of health, recreation, education, and social service providers directly targeting the needs of community residents. With a full-size indoor swimming pool, gymnasium, and nine club and fitness rooms, it is the prototype for future Chicago Park District facilities. In addition, a 20-room primary health care center is one of the largest providers of health services to uninsured patients in the city.

The Community Center, while serving current needs, also has deep-rooted connections to the past. Not only does the building rest on the original footings of the Sears catalog facility, but it extends the legacy of Sears founder Julius Rosenwald, who was famously generous in his support for YMCAs across the country. The Community Center campus is home to both a YMCA Child and Family Center and the state-of-the-art recreation facilities run by the Chicago Park District.

A number of visionary developers and investors are paving the way for the West Side complex of the 21st century. Over the next few years, more than $200 million of redevelopment will occur in the immediate area. Once again, the catalog plant facilities will become the center of community pride.

Homan Square is still a great location. Sears and Rosenwald's original buildings are still great structures. Economic and social upheaval are still great opportunities for bold solutions. Following is a series of photographs shown in chronological order to illustrate the evolution of the catalog plant complex during the past 100 years, including the overall grounds and advertising material.

LOOKING WEST ALONG HARVARD STREET, 1906. This early photograph shows open space along Harvard Street (renamed Arthington Street around 1914) and the Printing Building in the foreground, followed by the Administration and Merchandise Buildings. (Courtesy of the Chicago Historical Society.)

GENERAL VIEW OF THE GROUNDS STEREOGRAPH, 1906. In the foreground is the pergola, with the Administration and Merchandise Buildings shown on the left. The company claimed that it handled more printing and mailing activities than any other in the world at that time. The complex was described as being so large that it could be seen from passing trains six miles away. The Observation Tower provided views of the entire city on a reasonably clear day. (Courtesy of the Real Estate Capital Institute.)

HEADING TO WORK STEREOGRAPH, 1906. In this view, similar to the previous stereograph, employees dressed in Victorian clothes head west to work. The vast majority of workers appear to be women. (Courtesy of the Real Estate Capital Institute.)

CLOSING HOUR STEREOGRAPH, 1906. When the facilities closed at 5:30 p.m., streetcar lines and elevated railway companies made special provisions for handling more than 9,000 employees leaving the complex every day. (Courtesy of the Real Estate Capital Institute.)

SEARS, ROEBUCK AND CO. CATALOG, 1906. This full-cover back page illustrates a bird's-eye view of the new complex, including a 1.5-million-square-foot floor plan spanning five buildings. (Courtesy of the Real Estate Capital Institute.)

FOUNTAIN AND GARDEN AREA STEREOGRAPH, 1906. The gardens extend for a city block and the entire length of the Administration Building and printing plant along Harvard (Arthington) Avenue. The retailer claimed that this garden was one of the most beautiful spots in the whole city of Chicago. An artificial lake was originally constructed here with three fountains. Across the street was a greenhouse where thousands of flowers were grown, then planted in the garden. (Courtesy of the Real Estate Capital Institute.)

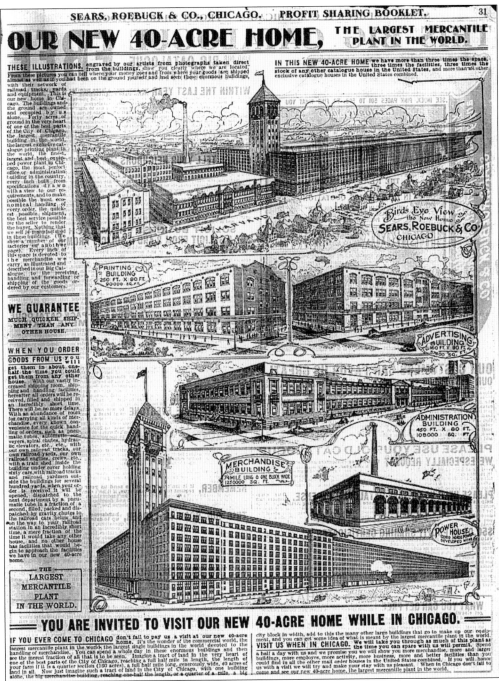

SEARS CATALOG COMPLEX DESCRIPTION, 1908. This section of the catalog emphasizes Sears's ownership of the property without any debt. A year earlier, the company took itself public by issuance of stock to help its extremely rapid expansion during this era. Henry Sachs (co-founder of Goldman Sachs) was the investment banker involved in this historically significant transition for Sears's conversion from private to public hands.

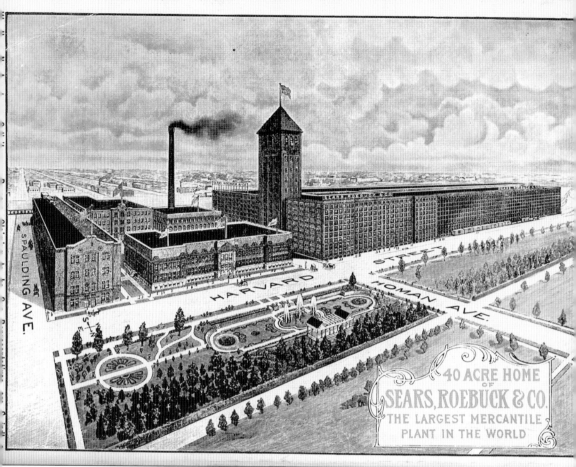

SEARS CATALOG, 1908. Once again, Sears prominently displays an aerial illustration of the complex on the back page of its catalog. By this time, the company claimed to be "the largest mercantile plant in the world." Compare this illustration to the 1906 illustration displaying vacant land in the foreground. (Courtesy of the Real Estate Capital Institute.)

Come and See Us When You Are in Chicago

OUR 40-ACRE PLANT, THE WORLD'S GREATEST MERCANTILE INSTITUTION.   SEE HOW TO REACH OUR PLANT, ON OTHER SIDE

SEARS, ROEBUCK AND CO.   -   -   CHICAGO, ILLINOIS

F6283   (OVER)

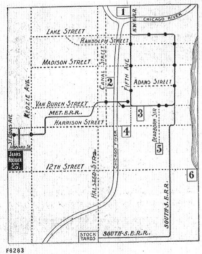

How to Reach Sears, Roebuck and Co.'s Plant

From Railroad Stations and Stock Yards

1—**Chicago and Northwestern Railroad Station.** Take Metropolitan Elevated Railroad (train marked "Garfield Park") at corner of Fifth Avenue and Randolph Street. Ask conductor to let you off at Sears, Roebuck and Co.'s plant.

2—**Union Station.** Take Metropolitan Elevated Railroad (train marked "Garfield Park") at Canal Street. Ask conductor to let you off at Sears, Roebuck and Co.'s plant.

3—**La Salle Street Station.** Take Metropolitan Elevated Railroad (train marked "Garfield Park"). Ask conductor to let you off at Sears, Roebuck and Co.'s plant.

4—**Grand Central Station.** Take Harrison Street car. Ask conductor to let you off at Sears, Roebuck and Co.'s plant.

5—**Dearborn (or Polk) Street Station.** Take Harrison Street car. Ask conductor to let you off at Sears, Roebuck and Co.'s plant.

6—**Illinois Central Station.** Take Twelfth Street car. Ask conductor to let you off at Sears, Roebuck and Co.'s plant.

FROM STOCK YARDS take Halsted Street car marked "Through Route No. 24," ask the conductor for a transfer ticket and to let you off at Harrison Street. Then take Harrison Street car and ask conductor to let you off at Sears, Roebuck and Co.'s plant.

(OVER)

F6283

"COME AND SEE US WHEN YOU ARE IN CHICAGO," 1906. This information card provides directions from downtown Chicago train stations to the Complex via surface streetcar. The facilities were so well known that visitors often asked conductors how to get to the property by name instead of address. (Courtesy of the Real Estate Capital Institute.)

A VISIT TO SEARS, ROEBUCK AND CO. CHICAGO BROCHURE, C. 1920. The cover page of this brochure features the original Sears Tower. Printed by Sears as a tour guide, it also describes the various activities performed within the complex and lists additional plants owned nationwide. (Courtesy of the Real Estate Capital Institute.)

Our employes enjoying open air concert, rendered by our 60-piece employes' band. During inclement weather, concerts are given Friday noons in the different rest rooms for the benefit of our employes. There are four rest rooms, one in each of our buildings, comfortably equipped, where employes may go to read, rest or enjoy music, as they themselves might provide.

PERGOLA, C. 1920. Seasonal activities in the garden area included live performances. The company had a 60-piece band play outdoor concerts. (Courtesy of the Real Estate Capital Institute.)

SEARS ATHLETIC FIELD EVENTS, c. 1920. Various sporting events, including women's dancing classes, were held in Sears Field. The company encouraged after-work social activities to maintain high morale. (Courtesy of the Real Estate Capital Institute.)

CLUBHOUSE AND TENNIS COURTS, c. 1920. Sears made every effort to encourage athletic activities. Two clubhouses—for both men and women—adjoined Sears Field and included showers and locker rooms. Also adjacent to Sears Field, 16 tennis courts were exclusively available to employees. (Courtesy of the Real Estate Capital Institute.)

VIEW OF ATHLETIC FIELD, SHOWING PART OF PLANT IN THE BACKGROUND

A strip of land one block wide and a half-mile long is devoted to the benefit of our employes. Many facilities are offered to employes to encourage athletic activities. This view shows the athletic field on the day of the annual Field Meet, which we tell you about on one of the following pages.

ANNUAL TRACK AND FIELD MEETS, C. 1920. The 10th Annual Track and Field meet is shown here. During its heyday of the first two decades, 20,000 people attended. (Courtesy of the Real Estate Capital Institute.)

A picture taken at our 10th Annual Track and Field Meet, showing a group of women employes in a long wand drill.

ATHLETIC SHOW, C. 1920. In this image, the women's long wand exhibition occurs and men sprint toward the finish line during the 10th Annual Track and Field Meet. (Courtesy of the Real Estate Capital Institute.)

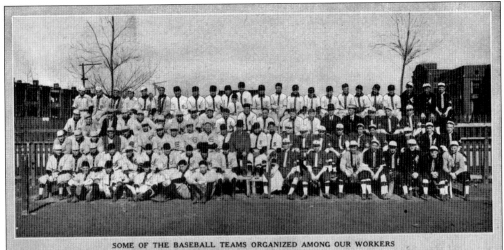

SOME OF THE BASEBALL TEAMS ORGANIZED AMONG OUR WORKERS
There are twelve baseball teams organized among our employes, six major and six minor teams. These teams play each other during the season and great interest is taken in the game. At the end of the season pennants are given to the teams with the highest standing.

BASEBALL TEAM, C. 1920. All team sports were promoted, with baseball being one of the most popular. A decade earlier, the Chicago Cubs had won two World Series less than a couple miles directly east of the complex in the West Side Ground (pre–Wrigley Field era). (Courtesy of the Real Estate Capital Institute.)

THE SEARS-ROEBUCK DEPARTMENT OF THE Y. M. C. A.
The Sears-Roebuck Department of the Y. M. C. A. adjoins our grounds to the northeast. It affords an ideal home for young men. It has three hundred rooms and is equipped with a swimming pool, gymnasium for men and boys, two large reading rooms, billiard rooms, bowling alleys and an excellent athletic field. This department is a branch of the Young Men's Christian Association of Chicago.

SEARS YMCA, C. 1920. In addition to events sponsored on company property, Sears also had a YMCA facility (still standing today) at the corner of Kedzie and Arthington Streets. (Courtesy of the Real Estate Capital Institute.)

SUNKEN GARDEN, LILY PAD, AND PERGOLA, C. 1923. The sunken gardens featured flower beds and a lily pond stocked with fish. Flowers were constantly in bloom, as non-blooming flowers were rotated or replaced with greenhouse-grown stock. (Courtesy of the Chicago Historical Society.)

SEARS ATHLETIC FIELD PARKING LOT, C. 1926. By the mid-1920s, automobile parking had overtaken the athletic field in terms of importance. A strategic shift in retailing from catalog to store sales accompanied the rapid growth of automobile ownership during this time, hastening the opening of the facility's first retail store. (Courtesy of the Homan Arthington Foundation.)

CLOSE-UP AERIAL VIEW OF CATALOG COMPLEX, 1936. This view looks northeast from Douglas Boulevard toward Sacramento Boulevard. By the 1930s, the half-mile-long facility covered over 50 acres. (Courtesy of the Chicago Historical Society.)

AERIAL VIEW OF CATALOG COMPLEX, 1936. The catalog complex is seen here within a quarter-mile radius. (Courtesy of the Chicago Historical Society.)

CATALOG PLANT CUTAWAY VIEW, 1943. This image provided the cover for an employee magazine about a city within a city. (Courtesy of the Real Estate Capital Institute.)

EASTSIDE SURFACE PARKING LOT, 1945. This parking lot was located at Kedzie and Arthington Streets (now occupied by the Allstate Building). (Courtesy of the Homan Arthington Foundation.)

ARTHINGTON STREET, 1940S. This view of Arthington Street looks southwest from the pergola. (Courtesy of the Homan Arthington Foundation.)

THE 3400 BLOCK ARTHINGTON PARKING LOT, 1945. This parking lot replaced the Sears Athletic Field. (Courtesy of the Homan Arthington Foundation.)

THE 900 BLOCK HOMAN AVENUE, 1945. This view of Homan Avenue looks north, with the Merchandise Building to the left and the Administration Building to the right. (Courtesy of the Homan Arthington Foundation.)

THE 3600 BLOCK ARTHINGTON STREET, 1945. Looking east toward the Merchandise Building, this view gives a clear indication of the structure's massive length. (Courtesy of the Homan Arthington Foundation.)

SEARS, ROEBUCK AND CO. COMPLEX EMPLOYEE ANNIVERSARY LAPEL PIN. The pin was given based on the 66th anniversary of the company. (Courtesy of the Homan Arthington Foundation.)

ARTHINGTON STREET LOOKING EAST, 1965. This mid-1960s view reveals the importance of the automobile, as structured parking replaced surface parking, which of course had replaced the athletic field a half-century earlier. (Courtesy of the Chicago Historical Society.)

CATALOG COMPLEX AERIAL, 1982. By the time of this southwestward view, Sears had vacated much of the complex but still maintained various warehouse and office operations here. (Courtesy of the Homan Arthington Foundation.)

HOMAN SQUARE, 1994. The 1990s ushered a new era, as Homan Square replaced much of the complex, including the Merchandise Building and the parking lots west of the Administration Building. (Courtesy of the Real Estate Capital Institute.)

AERIAL VIEW, 2002. This view is almost identical to those captured in photographs of the early 20th century. Note the absence of the Merchandise Building, dismantled in 1994. The preserved Tower is among the structures designated a federal and city landmark. (Courtesy of AirPhoto USA.)

COMPLEX AERIAL LOOKING WEST, 2002. This view, displaying the entire complex, looks to the west as far as Independence Boulevard—about a half-mile. The former Allstate Building is in the foreground, followed by the Printing Building, Administration Building, Power House, and Tower. Past the Tower is the Community Center, which now occupies the original Merchandise Building. To the left of the railroad tracks is the original wallpaper mill (now a Chicago Police Department facility) and to the right is the garden area. New housing replaces the parking lots and athletic fields of the past. The cul-de-sac is Boler Park, a municipal recreation area. (Courtesy of the Real Estate Capital Institute.)

COMPLEX AERIAL LOOKING EAST, 2002. Looking directly east, this view shows the complex. (Courtesy of the Real Estate Capital Institute.)

32

TOWER AND POWER HOUSE, 2003. The Tower and Power House, with the Administration Building beyond, are seen from the Community Center parking lot one block west. (Courtesy of the Real Estate Capital Institute.)

POWER HOUSE AERIAL VIEW, 2003. The Power House's 250-foot-high chimney dominates the foreground. The back of the Administration Building is clearly visible as well.

CATALOG COMPLEX CLOSE-UP AERIAL VIEW, 2003. This view, looking west toward the complex, reveals the massive size of the original and subsequent buildings. Well over 20 acres of floor space exists, including office, residential, commercial, recreational, and warehouse uses. Future plans call for more than three-quarters of the space to be converted to residential use, with much of the architectural beauty of the complex to remain intact. (Courtesy of the Real Estate Capital Institute.)

ROOF AREAS, 2003. Nearly six acres of the complex's roof area can be seen from the Observation Tower. (Courtesy of the Real Estate Capital Institute.)

RAILROAD RIGHT-OF-WAY SERVICE AREA, 2003. Much of the service area is exposed in this view, looking north from the tracks. Note the large heating and cooling equipment, added decades after original construction on the Printing Building. (Courtesy of the Real Estate Capital Institute.)

RAILROAD RIGHT-OF-WAY LOOKING EAST, 2003. Still in use today, the 1895 municipal water pumping station appears on the right in this image. Both original and current Sears Towers are visible in the background. (Courtesy of the Real Estate Capital Institute.)

HOMAN SQUARE AND THE CHICAGO SKYLINE, 2004. As seen from Boler Park, the Homan Square homes and the original Sears Tower are visible against the backdrop of Chicago. (Courtesy of the Real Estate Capital Institute.)

HOMAN SQUARE HOMES, 2003. On the former site of Sears Field, immediately northwest of the original Sears Tower, over 100 homes and apartments were built by the Shaw Company throughout the last decade. New development continues on the remaining lots. (Courtesy of the Real Estate Capital Institute.)

HOMAN SQUARE COMMUNITY CENTER, 2005. Standing on the vast site of the original three-million-square-foot Merchandise Building, the Community Center brings new life to the area. The center, built at a cost of over $28 million, is a state-of-the-art building with health care, community service, educational, and recreational facilities. This structure mirrors the original intentions of the complex's founders a century earlier: to ensure the safety and well-being of its occupants within the best facilities available. (Courtesy of the Real Estate Capital Institute.)

Sunken Gardens and Pergola, 2005. The gardens and pergola remain protected and preserved, looking virtually the same as a century earlier. The new owner plans to restore the pond and further expand the landscaping. On weekends, the gardens are often used for wedding photography. (Courtesy of the Real Estate Capital Institute.)

New Homes under Construction, 2005. In the heart of the Sears Athletic Field and what later became a parking lot, new single-family homes are being built. (Courtesy of Spyder Construction Company.)

Two

GREAT BUILDINGS

The distances in this picture are so great that the lens of the camera gets but a portion
of the great buildings in which are more than 50 acres of floor space devoted to our business.
—Sears, Roebuck and Co. stereograph brochure
referring to the Merchandise Building, 1906

In the midst of unbelievable and constant changes, four buildings have stood the test of time as lasting proof of the Sears catalog complex: the Administration Building, the original Sears Tower (the remaining structure of the Merchandise Building), the Catalog Press/Laboratory Building, and the Power House. Other surrounding buildings also exist, including the YMCA building (now a municipal agency), the wallpaper factory (a police headquarters), and a series of abandoned tunnels connecting the various structures. Furthermore, the pergola and gardens are so well preserved that one cannot tell the difference from a century ago.

Each of the buildings is a story in itself. Designed for commercial efficiency and enveloped by pleasing and classical architecture, these structures blend to form a true "city within a city." The sheer size and presence of the Tower and Administration Buildings represent a very unique community, offering a beautiful Victorian setting with state-of-the-art technologies, as seen in the world-class Homan Square Community Center.

The complex started with about 40 acres in 1906 and grew to more than 55 acres by the 1950s. It employed over 20,000 people by the mid-1920s, making it the largest private single-employment district in Illinois—true even today if it were in operation.

The following photographs, sorted in chronological order by building, cover these specific structures and other related properties that constituted the largest commercial complex of the era.

ADMINISTRATION BUILDING FOUNDATION UNDER CONSTRUCTION, 1905. In the earliest known photograph of the complex, footing is being placed. The Catalog Printing Buildings are well under construction, indicating move-in priority. (Courtesy of the Homan Arthington Foundation.)

ADMINISTRATION BUILDING WALLS UNDER CONSTRUCTION, 1905. Both horse-drawn and steam-powered equipment were used in the construction. The Power House and Catalog Printing Building are substantially completed, indicating move-in priority. (Courtesy of the Homan Arthington Foundation.)

BIRD'S-EYE VIEW OF THE NEW PLANT, SUMMER 1905. The complex was completed in record time, with an opening in January 1906. (Courtesy of the Homan Arthington Foundation.)

HARVARD (ARTHINGTON) STREET SCENE, C. 1906. This early photograph of the complex was likely taken in the summer during the noon hour. In the foreground is a horse-driven shuttle service. (Courtesy of the Homan Arthington Foundation.)

ADMINISTRATION BUILDING MAIN ENTRANCE STEREOGRAPH, 1906. This structure housed over 2,500 employees, including senior executives Richard Sears and Julius Rosenwald. A beehive of commercial bureaucracy, the original Administration Building (only three stories tall) covered about 3.5 acres of floor space. The first floor included the Auditing and Banking Departments, the second served as the Mail Opening and Mail Auditing Department, and the lower level provided dining and other employee services such as the Sereco Employee Mutual Benefit Society. "One of the striking features of this building is this wonderful arrangement of floors and offices, which are so laid out that the use of artificial light is seldom necessary," suggested company literature. (Courtesy of the Real Estate Capital Institute.)

PERGOLA STEREOGRAPH, 1906. The company identified this garden as "a popular retreat for our employees, and one of the most unique and decorative structures in Chicago. The quiet scene spread before you here is in striking contrast to the scenes of activity within the Administration Building. We believe these surroundings inspire our workers to better things and make for contentment and happiness." (Courtesy of the Real Estate Capital Institute.)

RETURNING FROM LUNCH, 1906. This noontime photograph was likely taken in July or August, as noted by the forest of umbrellas, common during that era as a form of protection from the sun. (Courtesy of the Real Estate Capital Institute.)

ADMINISTRATION BUILDING MAIN LOBBY, 1906. The lobby's builder commented, "Our Administration Building is one of the most perfect examples of modern architecture of our time. In quiet elegance we doubt whether this lobby is excelled in any building in the City of Chicago." The lobby is indeed the most striking illustration of the building's grandeur. The floors and wainscoting are marble, and at one time opalescent glass was built into the ceiling. (Courtesy of the Real Estate Capital Institute.)

CUSTOMER CORRESPONDENCE DEPARTMENT STEREOGRAPH, 1906. Here, employees wrote letters to customers. As many as 7,000 inquires were addressed daily. A variety of departments handled mail, including the Adjustment Inspection Department and the General Correspondence Department. (Courtesy of the Real Estate Capital Institute.)

CARD INDEX DEPARTMENT STEREOGRAPH, 1906. This large room was filled with filing cabinets in which records of all transactions were kept. Some 150 employees maintained these records using the index card as the base record format. The Sorting Division classified information according to state and town. The department was also responsible for updating customer records. (Courtesy of the Real Estate Capital Institute.)

MEN'S DINING ROOM STEREOGRAPH, 1906. Although the complex is mainly noted for merchandise distribution and catalog printing, its restaurant facilities were the largest in Chicago, and possibly the largest in the world. Prepared by more than 100 chefs, 12,000 meals were served daily, distributed through five restaurants. As was typical of the Victorian era, restaurants were divided into men's and women's facilities. Three meals could be eaten for 35¢ a day! (Courtesy of the Real Estate Capital Institute.)

WOMEN'S DINING ROOM STEREOGRAPH, 1906. During lunch hour, a single cafeteria could serve as many as 3,500 employees. The company was very proud of all these facilities, noting that "there is a splendid refrigerator controlled from our refrigerating plant." It was not until about 20 years later that the average household owned a refrigerator. (Courtesy of the Real Estate Capital Institute.)

AUTOMATIC TELEPHONE SWITCHBOARD STEREOGRAPH, 1906. This was one of the early forms of unattended telephone routing. (Courtesy of the Real Estate Capital Institute.)

LONG DISTANCE OPERATOR'S TELEPHONE SWITCHBOARD STEREOGRAPH, 1906. During the early years of the telephone network, the company operated a private plant equipped with telephones that were served by the now defunct Chicago Telephone Company. Long-distance connections to major markets in the country at that time included New York, Boston, St. Louis, Minneapolis, St. Paul, Cleveland, and Detroit. These markets were classified as all of the great cities of the East and West. Long-distance service was primarily used for contacting various factories and producers throughout the country, as very few customers had affordable access to private telephone service. Four operators manned the telephone equipment using 20 trunk lines, which provided 135 phones for the entire complex, an unbelievably low communication ratio considering that about 9,000 people worked at the plant. (Courtesy of the Real Estate Capital Institute.)

PNEUMATIC TUBE STATION STEREOGRAPH, 1906. This elaborate system of pressurized tubes allowed written communications to be sent throughout the buildings. Documents were transported in cartridges through tubes, allowing an order be processed within hours of being received in the complex. (Courtesy of the Real Estate Capital Institute.)

GREAT TUNNEL STEREOGRAPH, 1906. Originating in the Power House was a very complete and complex mile-long system of old underground tunnels constructed of concrete. Used to transport merchandise, utilities, and mail through the various buildings, the tunnels were also designed to keep the complex in operation in the event of a fire or disaster. The tunnels carried about 100 miles of piping, over 4,000 miles of copper wire, and 10 miles of heating and ventilation duct work. (Courtesy of the Real Estate Capital Institute.)

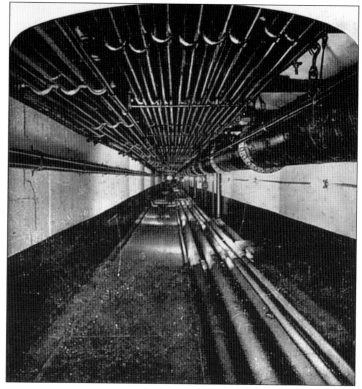

ADMINISTRATION BUILDING EXTERIOR AND COMPLEX, C. 1920. This foldout page of the Visit to Sears brochure features a bird's-eye view of the complex. By this time, the Administration Building included the three-floor addition, completed in 1914. (Courtesy of the Real Estate Capital Institute.)

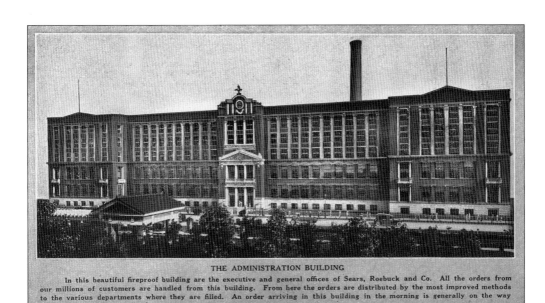

THE ADMINISTRATION BUILDING

In this beautiful fireproof building are the executive and general offices of Sears, Roebuck and Co. All the orders from our millions of customers are handled from this building. From here the orders are distributed by the most improved methods to the various departments where they are filled. An order arriving in this building in the morning is generally on the way to the customer the same day.

ADMINISTRATION BUILDING MAIN FAÇADE, C. 1923. Sears's catalog business rapidly expanded during the first decade of the facilities. In 1914, three floors were added without disturbing the architectural integrity of the building. Sears claimed to be able to process almost any order within 24 hours of receipt. (Courtesy of the Real Estate Capital Institute.)

EMPLOYES GOING HOME FROM WORK

There is an army of eighteen thousand men and women working in the buildings within our view and another army of twenty thousand in the factories and branches elsewhere. Considering the families depending on the employes for support, Sears, Roebuck and Co. daily provide for a large city.

CLOSING HOUR, C. 1920. Within two decades, the number of employees working at the complex doubled to nearly 20,000—the size of a small city. (Courtesy of the Real Estate Capital Institute.)

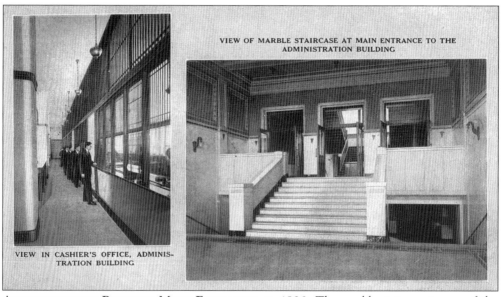

VIEW OF MARBLE STAIRCASE AT MAIN ENTRANCE TO THE ADMINISTRATION BUILDING

VIEW IN CASHIER'S OFFICE, ADMINISTRATION BUILDING

ADMINISTRATION BUILDING MAIN ENTRANCE, C. 1920. The marble staircase is one of the key features of the lobby, as is the bank facility located on the main floor. (Courtesy of the Real Estate Capital Institute.)

WAR MEMORIALS, C. 1923. Six bronze tablets installed in the Administration Building listed and honored all of the Sears employees serving in the military during World War I. (Courtesy of the Real Estate Capital Institute.)

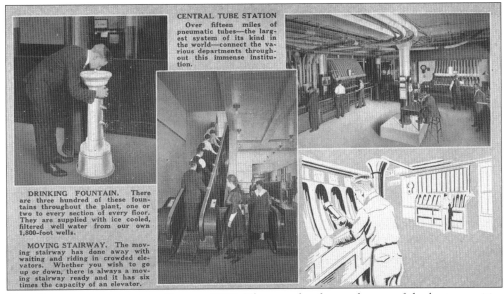

NEW TECHNOLOGIES OF THE DAY, C. 1920. The complex featured some of the best amenities of an office building during this time, including spring-fed water fountains, escalators, and compressed-air tubes for sending documents. (Courtesy of the Real Estate Capital Institute.)

MAIL OPENING and CASH ENTRY. From 1,500 to 3,000 pounds of mail, comprising 90,000 to 180,000 letters, are received here every day. The envelopes are stamped with the date and hour of receipt by a clever little machine which also cuts a fine strip from the top of the envelopes, opening them at the rate of 450 per minute. The mail opening clerks then dispose of the contents of the letters, the money going to the cashier, orders and inquiries to the auditor.

MAIL OPENING DEPARTMENT, C. 1920. In this department, serving as the entry point of all data, information was processed and filed manually. (Courtesy of the Real Estate Capital Institute.)

CORRESPONDENCE DEPARTMENT
The "Dictation" division of our Correspondence Department is shown in the above picture.

CORRESPONDENCE DEPARTMENT, C. 1920. This department was the focal point of database entry. (Courtesy of the Real Estate Capital Institute.)

INDEX AND ROUTING

Record cards of all orders are made out and filed under the full name of the customer, post office address, and the amount of money sent in. The orders are then "routed"—that is, the means of transportation is determined; if by parcel post, what zone; if by express, what company; if by freight, what railroad. The order is then passed on to the Distribution Department which makes out the "schedule"—the rate of progress each order must make through the various departments.

INDEXING DEPARTMENT, C. 1920. All correspondence was indexed and routed from this room. (Courtesy of the Real Estate Capital Institute.)

SCRIBING DEPARTMENT

The constant service of about three hundred clerks is required in this department for writing shipping labels, box markers and bills of lading; and when an order is to go by freight an acknowledgment card is sent to the customer from this division.

SCRIBING DEPARTMENT, C. 1920. More than 300 clerks handled shipping labels and documented mailing instructions for all catalog orders. (Courtesy of the Real Estate Capital Institute.)

BILLING DEPARTMENT, C. 1920. As customers' orders were processed, different sheets comprising the bill traveled via conveyor belt to the Billing Department. At this area, bills were distributed among about 400 clerks by conveyor belt and messengers to the shipping area in the Merchandise Building. (Courtesy of the Real Estate Capital Institute.)

CATALOG ADDRESSING DEPARTMENT, C. 1920. Addressing functions required substantial amounts of clerical labor and were highly efficient. (Courtesy of the Chicago Historical Society.)

VIEWS IN OUR CAFE-TEPIA

The Cafeteria and Restaurants are conducted as a part of our Service Department. In our Cafeteria alone, 3,500 employes wait on themselves and secure their lunches at nominal sums. A model kitchen is maintained; open for inspection at all times. In connection there is a splendid refrigerator controlled from our refrigerating

CAFETERIA SERVICE, C. 1920. The cafeteria was located on the lower level of the Administration Building. This type of dining was the predecessor to fast-food service, as it was popular throughout the first half of the 20th century. (Courtesy of the Real Estate Capital Institute.)

GRILL ROOM

In our restaurant, which consists of cafeteria lunch rooms, grill and dining rooms, over 6,000 employes are accommodated during the luncheon period, from 11:30 A. M. to 1:00 P. M. Breakfast is also served for all who so desire.

LUNCH ROOM

MAIN DINING ROOM

DINING ROOMS, C. 1920. This vast area covered at least an acre of space. (Courtesy of the Real Estate Capital Institute.)

RECREATION ROOM. Recreation and Lounging Room for our women employes. A Beckwith Artists' Concert Grand Piano and a Model XVI Silvertone Phonograph supply the music for games and dancing.

LIBRARY. Our Employes' Library has the largest circulation of all Commercial and Branch Libraries in the City of Chicago, averaging 50 periodicals and 400 books per day. In addition to the 8,000 volumes carried on open shelves, our employes may also obtain through this Library any book from the Chicago Public Library within twenty-four hours. One of our motor trucks makes daily trips for that purpose.

A VIEW IN THE LIBRARY

LIBRARY, C. 1920. The Administration Building's library was one of the most comprehensive privately owned and operated libraries in Chicago. Consistent with the company's priority of employee satisfaction, the library included a recreation room where workers could listen to records while resting. Sears also held reciprocity with the Chicago Public Library; therefore, books could be borrowed by employees and picked up and dropped off at the plant. (Courtesy of the Real Estate Capital Institute.)

CATALOG ORDERING DEPARTMENT, C. 1945. This department is seen during World War II. During this time, the overwhelming percentage of clerical laborers continued to be women. (Courtesy of the Chicago Historical Society.)

ARTHINGTON STREET, C. 1945. This view of the Administration Building looks east from Homan Avenue. (Courtesy of the Homan Arthington Foundation.)

LEAVING WORK, C. 1945. Employees depart for home. Like the one above, this view looks west from Spaulding Avenue. (Courtesy of the Homan Arthington Foundation.)

This is Sears "West Side"

Covering 37 acres, it is the world's largest mercantile plant

ADMINISTRATION BUILDING MAIN ENTRANCE, 1964. This photograph was taken at the peak of Sears's retail dominance while at this location. (Courtesy of the Sears Archives.)

ADMINISTRATION BUILDING MAIN ENTRANCE, 2005. In this close-up view, the building appears virtually unchanged since its 1914 expansion. (Courtesy of the Real Estate Capital Institute.)

ARTHINGTON STREET, 2005. The Administration Building's entire front façade is shown here. Little has changed in this view. (Courtesy of the Real Estate Capital Institute.)

HOMAN AVENUE, 2005. This image depicts the intersection of Homan Avenue and Arthington Street. (Courtesy of the Real Estate Capital Institute.)

PRESIDENT'S OFFICE, 2005. Richard Sears's office is revealed in this view. (Courtesy of the Real Estate Capital Institute.)

SECRETARY'S OFFICE, 2005. This area served as the office lobby for executives. (Courtesy of the Real Estate Capital Institute.)

BOARDROOM, 2005. Business people gathered here to make major decisions. The formation of Allstate Insurance and the construction of the Sears Tower are among the highlights of events decided here. (Courtesy of the Real Estate Capital Institute.)

MAIN ENTRANCE, 2005. The Administration Building has remained well preserved during the past century. (Courtesy of the Real Estate Capital Institute.)

AERIAL VIEW, 2005. Looking southwest toward the original Sears Tower, this view shows the shaded markings of the Administration Building. (Courtesy of the Real Estate Capital Institute.)

MERCHANDISE BUILDING MAIN ENTRANCE, 1906. The most recognizable structure within the plant was primarily known as the Merchandise Building; however, the structure also had other frequently used names including the Catalog Building, the Tower, and the Works, as most of the merchandise manufacturing and handling was done here. Upon completion, the structure was believed to be the largest commercial building in the world, with over three million square feet of space. The tower portion was the tallest building in the city outside of downtown, peaking at 250 feet. The merchandise handling area spanned over a quarter-mile and reached nine stories. The Merchandise Building, in effect, was America's mail-order mall. The facility stocked more than $8 million of inventory. And it used over 28 million bricks, 25,000 barrels of lime, 130,000 barrels of cement, and 15 million feet of lumber—enough to consume a 3,000-acre forest. (Courtesy of the Chicago Historical Society.)

FRONT SECTION, EARLY 1900S. The Merchandise Building was too large to photograph in its entirety, so the front section and Tower became the most recognizable. (Courtesy of the Real Estate Capital Institute.)

RAIL YARD AND SOUTH ELEVATION STEREOGRAPH, 1906. Because the complex delivered merchandise to almost all sections of the country, no individual railroad line could offer such distribution capacity. The solution was to locate the site adjacent to the Chicago Terminal Transfer Railway. Based on this arrangement, nearly all railroads (except two) were directly accessible to the facility. One side of the Merchandise Building served as the receiving depot, while the other served as the shipping point. Engine and train crews worked 24 hours a day in handling the rail traffic at the complex. (Courtesy of the Real Estate Capital Institute.)

FIRE DEPARTMENT DRILL STEREOGRAPH, 1906. Although the city of Chicago provided fire protection, the size and scale of the complex created special needs for a "city within a city." A private fire department, naturally, was one of the necessities required for an effective life-safety program. The company created a special fire-fighting crew with an independent water supply to watch over the expansive operation. Daily fire drills were practiced by this volunteer department. The buildings were also well ahead of their time by featuring a total of 60,000 automatic sprinkler systems. (Courtesy of the Real Estate Capital Institute.)

MERCHANDISE BUILDING, MAIN ENTRANCE, 1906. These employees are entering work. (Courtesy of the Real Estate Capital Institute.)

MEN'S CLOTHING FACTORY STEREOGRAPH, 1906. The top floor of the Merchandise Building (nine floors, exclusive of the tower) served as the clothing manufacturing facility within the complex. This floor featured ample daylight through its large windows and skylights. The company boasted that it was the finest clothing manufacturing plant of its kind in the world. As many as 6,000 clothing orders were processed per day. (Courtesy of the Real Estate Capital Institute.)

MUSIC RECORD AREA STEREOGRAPH, 1906. This area served as the storage room for sound records. Originally known as "talking machine records," records played on the gramophone were among the most popular items sold by the retailer. Sears claimed to be the largest dealer of talking machines and records in the country. (Courtesy of the Real Estate Capital Institute.)

TRAIN SHED STEREOGRAPH, 1906. The train shed and seven-acre shipping rooms were the nerve center of the Merchandise Building. Orders were handled in the Administration Building and delivered to the various departments and floors of the Merchandise Building through a system of pneumonic tubes. The ninth floor manufactured clothing, the seventh floor jewelry, and the fourth floor cameras. Orders above the second floor were processed and delivered using an intricate system of old speed-regulated gravity chutes. According to promotional literature, "This process is very rapid and goods are disposed of about as rapidly as if they were thrown out the window." Even glass merchandise could be delivered without breakage. Heavy goods were stored on the lower floor and delivered via traveling conveyors. (Courtesy of the Real Estate Capital Institute.)

SHIPPING AREA STEREOGRAPH, 1906. Goods were delivered and packaged here to be loaded onto railcars. (Courtesy of the Real Estate Capital Institute.)

TRAINING SCHOOL STEREOGRAPH, 1906. Located in the Merchandise Tower, the training school included four floors of classroom programs for stenography, typing, dictation, and overall material-handling technologies. Programs ranged from three days to three weeks. (Courtesy of the Real Estate Capital Institute.)

MERCHANDISE BUILDING

The greatest of all the buildings in our plant is the Merchandise Building. It is 1,223 feet long, 310 feet wide, and nine stories high, and has a tower 225 feet high, which gives a splendid view of Chicago and a panorama of the entire plant of Sears, Roebuck & Co. Throughout the building there are rows of shelves and bins filled ceiling high with merchandise in packages, according to the way it is quoted in the catalog; tickets take the place of customers, and silently and rapidly the clerks are filling the orders. The order simply reads so much of this and so much of that; the stock is all ready and the clerks do the rest, filling scores of orders at one trip through the department. These are conveyed to a gravity chute through which they are quickly dispatched to the Shipping Department on a lower floor.

MERCHANDISE BUILDING EXTERIOR, C. 1920. Part of the Visit to Sears brochure, this image gives a majestic view of the largest commercial building in the world at the time. (Courtesy of the Real Estate Capital Institute.)

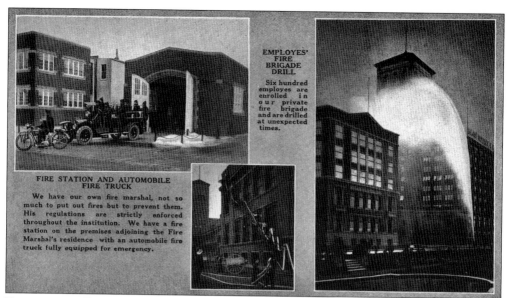

FIREFIGHTING DRILL, C. 1920. A private fire station was built across the street from the complex. (Courtesy of the Real Estate Capital Institute.)

TRUCK AND RAIL DOCKS, C. 1920. Rail traffic moved merchandise, while trucks shipped mail. (Courtesy of the Real Estate Capital Institute.)

Interior views of the Modern Bungalow exhibited in our Mill Work and Building Material Department.

View showing Living Room and Dining Room with Colonial Interior Columns.

The designs shown here are those approved by the leading architects of the country. The proportions are graceful, massive and dignified. Our bungalows are built from properly seasoned and beautifully finished lumber according to the most modern plans.

View of a Corridor showing a few of the many glass doors, staircases and consoles sold in our Millwork Department.

MILLWORK OFFICE, C. 1920. This area was used for displaying interior home components, similar to today's home improvement centers. (Courtesy of the Real Estate Capital Institute.)

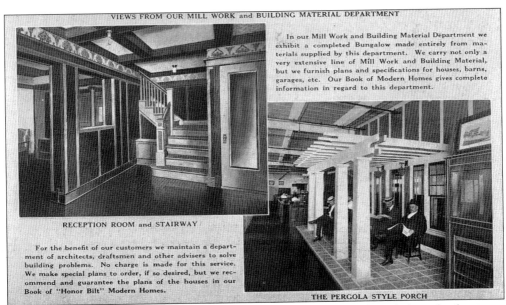

VIEWS FROM OUR MILL WORK and BUILDING MATERIAL DEPARTMENT

In our Mill Work and Building Material Department we exhibit a completed Bungalow made entirely from materials supplied by this department. We carry not only a very extensive line of Mill Work and Building Material, but we furnish plans and specifications for houses, barns, garages, etc. Our Book of Modern Homes gives complete information in regard to this department.

RECEPTION ROOM and STAIRWAY

For the benefit of our customers we maintain a department of architects, draftsmen and other advisers to solve building problems. No charge is made for this service. We make special plans to order, if so desired, but we recommend and guarantee the plans of the houses in our Book of "Honor Bilt" Modern Homes.

THE PERGOLA STYLE PORCH

SAMPLE HOUSE, C. 1920. Complete house interiors were exhibited, including the furniture, fixtures, and lighting. (Courtesy of the Real Estate Capital Institute.)

EXPRESS COMPANIES' OF-
FICES and MOTOR TRUCKS. All
the leading Railroad Express Companies have offices in our plant.
Express packages coming down
the chute from our express packers are received and inspected by
clerks in this department and as-
signed to the clerks of the various express companies designated
by the Routing Department. The
express companies' clerks re-
check these packages against the
shipping tickets, weigh the packages and put down the amount of
the charges, then send them out
on roller trucks to their motor
trucks outside.

EXPRESS MAIL ROUTING AND TERMINALS, C. 1920. American Express and the Railway Express Agency were the early pioneers of shipping packages via truck for more rapid delivery. (Courtesy of the Real Estate Capital Institute.)

FREIGHT SORTING

The Steel Link Conveyor mentioned below brings the boxes to the freight sorters, who inspect the markings on the boxes and assign them to the proper railroads for shipment. There is a separate place for the merchandise to be shipped by each rail-road and every railroad entering Chicago is represented.

FREIGHT PACKING

Merchandise intended for freight shipment, on being sent down the chutes from the Relay Platform previously mentioned, reaches the receiving clerks in the Freight Packing Department, who assemble the various items into complete orders and dis-tribute them among the packers. The packers work in pairs; one puts the merchandise into the box, the other nails on the lid, pastes on the shipping tag or label, and places the box on the steel link conveyor.

FREIGHT SORTING DEPARTMENT, C. 1920. Freight was sorted according to railroad company. In this photograph, the Santa Fe, Marquette, and Grand Trunk Railroads are represented. (Courtesy of the Real Estate Capital Institute.)

SORTING AND ASSEMBLING

Gravity and belt conveyors, some of them two blocks long, bring here endless streams of moving baskets of merchandise. Here the baskets are assorted according to their modes of shipment, whether by parcel post, express or freight, then sent off on roller conveyors to the Relay Platform, where the different baskets belonging to each order are assembled and sent down gravity chutes to the various packers.

THE "TRIPPERS"

Perhaps the most ingenious machines devised for saving time in the handling of parcel post packages are the "Trippers." They travel up and down all day long, dropping to the right and left the packages fed to them by the endless belt conveyors.

EXPRESS MAIL ROUTING AND TERMINALS, C. 1920. Merchandise was delivered to the mail room via an ingenious conveyor belt and chute system, which operated 24 hours a day. (Courtesy of the Real Estate Capital Institute.)

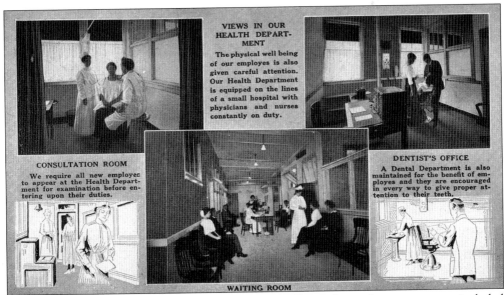

VIEWS IN OUR HEALTH DEPARTMENT

The physical well being of our employes is also given careful attention. Our Health Department is equipped on the lines of a small hospital with physicians and nurses constantly on duty.

CONSULTATION ROOM

We require all new employes to appear at the Health Department for examination before entering upon their duties.

DENTIST'S OFFICE

A Dental Department is also maintained for the benefit of employes and they are encouraged in every way to give proper attention to their teeth.

WAITING ROOM

HEALTH CARE FACILITIES, C. 1920. A hospital, dental office, and consultation room were included for job screenings and employee safety. (Courtesy of the Real Estate Capital Institute.)

Anne and Sue Bring Tower Topics

Anne Williams and Sue Roberts claim the distinction of having the only household program for men on the air in the Middle West. It comes on Tower Topics Time from the Sears, Roebuck and Company studio each Monday morning. Other Tower Topics features are recipes, child welfare, neighborly news, decorating shop and Junior Time.

"Tom and Alice Burke" are eagerly looked forward to by thousands on Sears-Roebuck Matinee Time each Friday afternoon. This one-hour program also brings pleasing numbers of the Maple City Four, Grace Wilson, other artists. A shoppers' service program by Sue and Anne on Monday and Wednesday afternoons is another Sears feature.

The Sears, Roebuck Agricultural Foundation, Edw. J. Condon, Director, arranges all programs from the Tower Studio.

Sue Roberts. Her specialty is home decoration and she had direct charge of the "Home Beautiful" contest with its tens of thousands of entries. She is a Chicago girl and attended Northwestern University.

Anne Williams calls Springfield, Illinois, her home town and she is a graduate of the University of Illinois. Anne is a specialist in women's styles and makes trips to New York twice a year to get acquainted with the newest fashions. Yes—she has a husband. She has been heard on WLS for about four years.

Meet Grace Wilson, the "Bringing Home the Bacon" girl. She was one of our first artists on WLS and now appears regularly on Sears programs. Grace can sing "blues" and "sweet" songs with equal appeal. Each broadcast brings her numerous requests.

RADIO STATION, C. 1924. WLS Radio, an acronym for "World's Largest Store," started on the Tower's 11th floor. The station provides Sears's rural customers with crop and weather information. Later entertainment was added, including barn dance music. Singer Gene Autrey broadcasted from the facilities in the early years. (Courtesy of the WLS Radio Web site.)

FIRST RETAIL STORE, C. 1926. Sears understood the changes brought about by the automobile and began opening retail outlets for customers to drive to instead of solely relying on mail order. (Courtesy of the Sears Archives Web site.)

HOMAN AVENUE, C. 1945. The north side of the Merchandise Building is seen from Homan Avenue and the parking lot. By World War II, the entire Sears Athletic Field had been converted to surface parking. (Courtesy of the Homan Arthington Foundation.)

ARTHINGTON STREET, C. 1945. This view of Arthington Street looks west from Homan Avenue, with the complex on the left and the parking lot (former Sears Field) on the right. (Courtesy of the Homan Arthington Foundation.)

MERCHANDISE BUILDING TOWER, C. 1980. By this time, the Merchandise Building was only used on a limited basis as ancillary distribution space. (Courtesy of the Sears Archives Web site.)

MERCHANDISE BUILDING CENTRAL SECTION, C. 1992. Taken from the parking lot along Arthington Street, this photograph shows the building's central area. (Courtesy of the Real Estate Capital Institute.)

MORAN SKYWALK, C. 1992. This bridge linked the former wallpaper plant (one block south on Fillmore Street) to the Catalog Building by crossing Homan Avenue. (Courtesy of the Real Estate Capital Institute.)

MERCHANDISE BUILDING SOUTH SECTION, C. 1992. This view, taken prior to demolition and redevelopment, looks along Homan Avenue and the railroad embankment. (Courtesy of the Real Estate Capital Institute.)

HOMAN AND ARTHINGTON INTERSECTION, C. 1992. The merchandise warehouse section is pictured here prior to Homan Square's redevelopment. (Courtesy of the Real Estate Capital Institute.)

ORIGINAL SEARS TOWER NIGHTTIME VIEW, 1998. This view of the Tower was taken soon after redevelopment of the Merchandise Building land. Note the metal grid surrounding the Tower and reaching nine floors. Oftentimes, this grid is mistaken as a structural brace; instead, it represents the original Merchandise Building footprint as an architectural tribute. (Courtesy of the Homan Arthington Foundation.)

ORIGINAL SEARS TOWER DAYTIME VIEW, 2005. Looking southwest from Homan Avenue, this view reveals the metal bracing surrounding three sides of the building. (Courtesy of the Real Estate Capital Institute.)

ORIGINAL SEARS TOWER OBSERVATION DECK, 2005. This section has remained remarkably well preserved. Note the missing extended balcony, removed years earlier. (Courtesy of the Real Estate Capital Institute.)

MAIN ENTRANCE, 2005. "Homan Square" is currently inscribed on the front entrance of the original Sears Tower. The structure is now commonly known as the Homan Square Tower or the original Sears Tower. (Courtesy of the Real Estate Capital Institute.)

ABANDONED TUNNEL, 2005. This is just one of the many abandoned underground tunnels still found in the complex today. (Courtesy of the Real Estate Capital Institute.)

FIRST FLOOR, 2005. Soon to be redeveloped into loft-style residential and/or commercial space, the floors allow ample natural light. (Courtesy of the Real Estate Capital Institute.)

TYPICAL FLOOR, 2005. This floor was formerly used as the training school for office workers. The 12th and 13th floors are more unusual, as they are combined with a ceiling height of 38 feet. This combined floor was originally used for storing about 200,000 gallons of water for the complex sprinkler system. (Courtesy of the Real Estate Capital Institute.)

OBSERVATION DECK, 2005. The 14th floor was used by company executives for special functions, including greeting dignitaries. It provides views of the city from all directions. (Courtesy of the Real Estate Capital Institute.)

PERGOLA VIEW STEREOGRAPH, 1906. The Printing Building is hidden to the left of the Administration Building. (Courtesy of Real Estate Capital Institute.)

PRINTING BUILDING TYPESETTING STEREOGRAPH, 1906. Over 100 skilled printers set the type for the company catalogs, blank forms, and stationery. Each catalog averaged about 1,200 pages with nearly 100,000 price quotations and 10,000 illustrations. Throughout most of the 20th century, the Sears catalog was the largest mail-order catalog in existence. Its authors claimed "not to waste a single inch of paper;" therefore, smaller type and a crowding of information were common. (Courtesy of the Real Estate Capital Institute.)

CATALOG TRIMMING MACHINE STEREOGRAPH, 1906. Shown here is one of two machines known as Continuous Catalogue Trimmers. Roughly finished print was trimmed by these vast machines, which could handle 20,000 catalogs per day. (Courtesy of the Real Estate Capital Institute.)

AUTOMATIC GATHERING MACHINE STEREOGRAPH, 1906. This equipment gathered different sections of the catalog and arranged them in their proper order. The machine could also automatically discover any missing pages and monitor imperfections during the printing process. Specially built for the retailer, it was said to be the largest Gathering Machine of its time. (Courtesy of the Real Estate Capital Institute.)

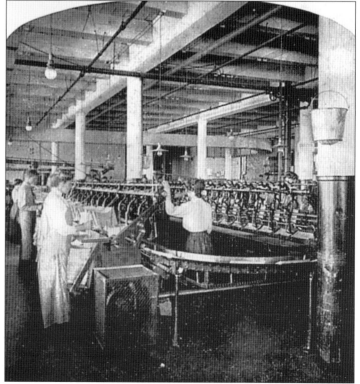

ELECTROTYPE FOUNDRY STEREOGRAPH, 1906.
A major technical advancement of the era focused on printing from electroplates instead of actual type. As a result, the volume and cost of printing catalogs became a mere fraction of such costs a few decades earlier. Without question, such an advancement allowed Sears to become one of the most cost-effective retailers in the country. (Courtesy of the Real Estate Capital Institute.)

PRINTING ROOM STEREOGRAPH, 1906. The "Big Catalog" was printed here. Believed to be the largest press room in the world, the Printing Building was a technological marvel. All of the equipment within the facility operated on electricity, which was rapidly replacing steam technology as the preferred form of powering machinery. The amount of paper processed could reportedly be wrapped around the world nearly 10 times. Approximately six million catalogs were sent out annually during the early years of the operation. (Courtesy of the Real Estate Capital Institute.)

TYPE MAKING STEREOGRAPH, 1906. This image provides a detailed view of typesetting and type making. (Courtesy of the Real Estate Capital Institute.)

MONOTYPE AND LINOTYPE MACHINES

VIEWS IN THE COMPOSING ROOM

The Composing Room is where the type is set for our large General Catalog, our Special Catalogs and thousands of pieces of miscellaneous job work. It is the largest private composing room in the United States. About 300 compositors, linotype and monotype machine operators and proofreaders are here engaged in setting up the type, making up the pages and reading and checking the finished pages.

PRESS ROOM STEREOGRAPH, 1920. A corner of the press room is pictured here. The photograph caption states, "The invention of typesetting machines and rotary printing presses has cheapened the production of newspapers, periodicals and books and has placed the finest literature of the ages within the reach of those in the most moderate circumstances. Probably no industry of our time has made more rapid strides than the printing industry and it is even now undergoing great and important changes." (Courtesy of Real Estate Capital Holdings.)

ARTHINGTON STREET, C. 1920. Looking west along Arthington Street, this view shows a greenhouse to the left and open field area. The Printing Building stands in the background. (Courtesy of the Chicago Historical Society.)

ADVERTISING AND PRINTING BUILDING AND ANNEX

The L-shaped six-story Advertising and Printing Building and the four-story Annex, in all, houses one of the largest printing plants in America. This plant is equipped throughout with specially designed machinery for making and handling our tremendous yearly output of over 65,000,000 large catalogs, special sales books, special catalogs and other mailing matter.

PRINTING BUILDING OPEN VIEW, C. 1920. This image, part of the Visit to Sears brochure, displays how the facility would look if unobstructed by the Administration Building. (Courtesy of the Real Estate Capital Institute.)

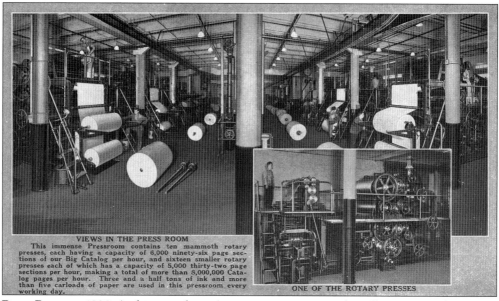

RESEARCH LABORATORY, C. 1920. By the 1920s, the Printing Building began serving the dual role of print shop and research lab. Sears was one of the first companies to take product research to heart, as the company promised full satisfaction with its merchandise and wanted to maintain quality control. (Courtesy of the Real Estate Capital Institute.)

PRESS ROOM, C. 1920. At this time, the press room was generating eight million pages per hour. Over three carloads of paper were consumed per day. (Courtesy of the Real Estate Capital Institute.)

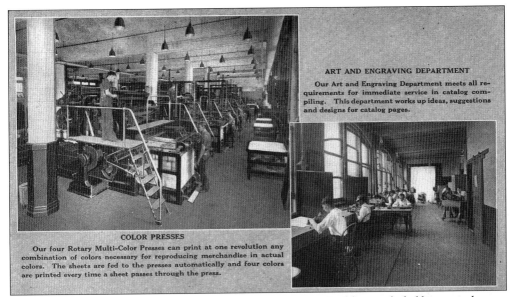

ART AND ENGRAVING DEPARTMENT, C. 1920. The Printing Building included large windows to permit maximum lighting for artists and printing operations such as that shown here. (Courtesy of the Real Estate Capital Institute.)

FOLDING OPERATIONS, C. 1920. Folding machines were used for regular catalogs, while manual folding was still employed for special mailings. (Courtesy of the Real Estate Capital Institute.)

GATHERING AND BINDING MACHINES

We use for the assembling of the different sections of the catalog three specially designed, 50-section gathering machines and four automatic binding and covering machines. The gathering machine is unique in its construction on account of its capacity of 2,000 perfect books per hour, which we obtain by having attached to it an ingenious device in the form of a pair of feelers which feel each section before it is dropped into the book to see that no pages are missing.

BINDING MACHINES

GATHERING AND BINDING MACHINES, C. 1920. Assembly line automation was used throughout all buildings of the complex. (Courtesy of the Real Estate Capital Institute.)

PRINTING BUILDING FAÇADE DETAIL, 2005. The façade incorporated decorative terra-cotta relating to research and printing technology. (Courtesy of the Real Estate Capital Institute.)

POWER HOUSE ENGINE ROOM STEREOGRAPH, 1906. Upon completion, the Power House was the largest commercially owned structure of its type in the world, with a floor plan of about three quarters of an acre. All of the main mechanical equipment was located on the first floor. Connecting pipes and automatic equipment were located below grade. The engine room was extremely ornamental, finished throughout with white-enameled brick and red English tile for the floor. (Courtesy of the Real Estate Capital Institute.)

BOILER ROOM STEREOGRAPH, 1906. The boilers could handle about 12,000 horsepower. Yet another marvel of efficiency, they were specially designed to recycle material by using smokeless furnaces to create energy from waste paper and refuse. Coal-carrying machinery, including a small railroad, had the capacity to process 100 tons per hour. (Courtesy of the Real Estate Capital Institute.)

"GREAT SWITCHBOARD" STEREOGRAPH, 1906. The Great Switchboard was an early example of one of the largest electrical control stations of the early 20th century. Described by Sears as "a wonderful advancement made in electrical science," the device was far ahead of its time, as it monitored not only electrical output but life and safety systems. (Courtesy of the Real Estate Capital Institute.)

RAIL YARD, 1914. Freight yards brought coal and oil to the Power House, in addition to deliveries. (Courtesy of the Sears Archives.)

SPECIAL POLICE PROVIDED FOR THE SAFETY OF OUR EMPLOYES.

POWER HOUSE

Our own Power House generates enough electricity for light and power to supply a fair size city. It not only supplies the enormous quantity of light and power needed for the plant, but also compressed air for the pneumatic tube system, refrigeration plant and water pumps.

POWER HOUSE MAIN FAÇADE, C. 1920. This view, appearing in the Visit to Sears brochure, displays a virtually identical façade to today. The company employed its own private police force. (Courtesy of the Real Estate Capital Institute.)

VIEW OF REFRIGERATING PLANT

Daily Capacity one hundred tons of ice. Fifty tons used for cooling the drinking water, and fifty tons used for grocery department.

ELEVEN BOILERS

Equipped with self-feeding chain grates. Twelve hundred tons of coal stored directly above boilers. The power house consumes on an average two hundred tons of coal a day. With our machinery we can handle a carload of coal in forty-five minutes.

AIR COMPRESSORS AND FIRE PUMPS

There are four air compressors with a capacity of 4,000 cubic feet per minute at 100 pounds pressure per square inch. The compressed air is used for operating our two 1,800 feet deep wells and for house uses. Seven large pumps are used with a capacity of 5,500 gallons per minute for fire duty and 2,000 additional gallons per minute for drinking purposes and other house uses.

POWER HOUSE PIPING, C. 1920. Air compressors and fire pumps tapped into the company's private 1,800-foot-deep well for water supply. The massive boiler room still exists today. (Courtesy of the Real Estate Capital Institute.)

POWER HOUSE, REAR VIEW, 2002. The rear view is seen from the Printing and Administration Buildings. (Courtesy of the Real Estate Capital Institute.)

RAILROAD COAL UNLOADING ZONE, 2002. Viewed from the railroad embankment, this area has not been used in years. (Courtesy of the Real Estate Capital Institute.)

POWER HOUSE FAÇADE DETAIL, 2002. As with other buildings in the complex, this ornate façade gives viewers an idea of the facility's function. (Courtesy of the Real Estate Capital Institute.)

GREAT SWITCHBOARD WALL, 2002. Of all of the buildings within the complex, this one has experienced the least amount of visible change. This area originally housed the Great Switchboard. (Courtesy of the Real Estate Capital Institute.)

GENERATOR ROOM, 2002. Although the actual equipment was updated throughout the years, the building's layout remained the same. (Courtesy of the Real Estate Capital Institute.)

STEAM GAUGE, 2002. Many of the gauges, pipes, and other equipment date back to the original construction. Equipment was extremely well maintained. Generations of operator-families traced their roots to this facility. (Courtesy of the Real Estate Capital Institute.)

ABANDONED BOILER, 2002. Some equipment outlived its useful life but was too costly to remove. (Courtesy of the Real Estate Capital Institute.)

HOMAN AVENUE, 2005. The Power House is viewed from the Homan Square Community Center. (Courtesy of the Real Estate Capital Institute.)

VISITOR'S GALLERY, 2005. Seen here is the visitor's gallery for viewing the steam and electric generating equipment. This area features brass rail construction. (Courtesy of the Real Estate Capital Institute.)

POWER HOUSE ENTRANCEWAY, 2005. The main entrance is located off of Homan Avenue. (Courtesy of the Real Estate Capital Institute.)

Our six-story Grocery Building with its seven acres of floor space is an imposing institution in itself. Built of steel ribbed poured concrete, it is a splendid example of the most modern type of fire-proof construction. Modern heating and cooling plants under perfect control supply the exact temperatures suitable for the various food products; while a ventilating system of the latest design prevents the odor of one kind of food from affecting another; and the air is kept free from dust by the vacuum cleaning process. The basement is arranged into separate rooms built especially for storing provisions requiring different temperatures, meats, dried fruits, dairy products, pickled goods, honey, syrups, bottled goods and the like. More than 6,000 carloads of groceries were shipped from this building during the past year.

GROCERY BUILDING

GROCERY BUILDING, C. 1920. Just west of the plant, the company owned a six-story building with seven acres of fire-proof floor space and innovative climate and odor control. From here, Sears shipped over 6,000 carloads of groceries during peak operations. (Courtesy of the Real Estate Capital Institute.)

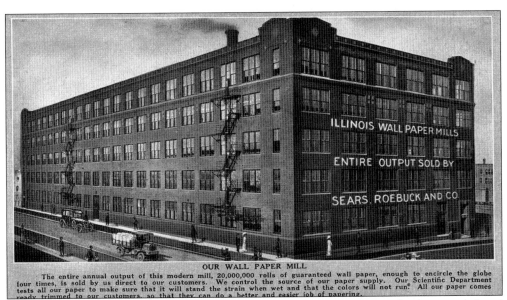

OUR WALL PAPER MILL

The entire annual output of this modern mill, 20,000,000 rolls of guaranteed wall paper, enough to encircle the globe four times, is sold by us direct to our customers. We control the source of our paper supply. Our Scientific Department tests all our paper to make sure that it will stand the strain when wet and that the colors will not run. All our paper comes ready trimmed to our customers, so that they can do a better and easier job of papering.

WALLPAPER FACTORY, C. 1920. Situated just south of the Power House, the factory produced enough wallpaper to circle around the world more than four times. (Courtesy of the Real Estate Capital Institute.)

TENT AND TRUNK FACTORY, C. 1920. This was one of the many manufacturing facilities in close proximity to the plant. (Courtesy of the Real Estate Capital Institute.)

PARKING STRUCTURE, C. 1960. Along with others, this structured parking lot was built after World War II to accommodate greater traffic loads. (Courtesy of the Chicago Historical Society.)

ALLSTATE...

ONE OF AMERICA'S LARGEST AND FASTEST GROWING AUTOMOBILE INSURANCE COMPANIES

Great Growth through Great Service

The New Home Office Building
of the Allstate Insurance Company
Chicago, Illinois

Founded by SEARS, ROEBUCK AND CO.
to give you
the utmost in Auto Insurance Service

ALLSTATE **INSURANCE COMPANY**
Specialists in Auto Insurance

A wholly owned subsidiary of Sears, Roebuck and Co. with assets
and liabilities distinct and separate from the parent company

DRIVE SAFELY...ONE OF THE LIVES YOU SAVE MAY BE YOUR OWN

ALLSTATE ADVERTISEMENT, C. 1950. A *Saturday Evening Post* full-page advertisement announces the new structure. Built in 1949, the Allstate Building is believed to be the first major postwar skyscraper built in Chicago, predating the Prudential Building by five years. (Courtesy of the Real Estate Capital Institute.)

ALLSTATE BUILDING PARKING STRUCTURE, 2005. A 1,100-car parking lot was built directly east of the pergola area. (Courtesy of the Real Estate Capital Institute.)

ALLSTATE TYPICAL FAÇADE, 2005. A skyway attached this structure to the Printing Building. (Courtesy of the Real Estate Capital Institute.)

ALLSTATE ENTRANCE, 2005. The Allstate Building is currently vacant. (Courtesy of the Real Estate Capital Institute.)

CHICAGO POLICE BUILDING, 2005. The former wallpaper factory now serves as evidence storage and special services for Chicago Police operations. (Courtesy of the Real Estate Capital Institute.)

HOMAN SQUARE COMMUNITY CENTER ENTRANCE, 2005. Developed by Charles H. Shaw, this community building includes a health care center, recreational facilities (pool, basketball courts), meeting rooms, a computer training center, and a cafe. It was also one of the first facilities to offer free wireless internet access to residents in the city. (Courtesy of the Real Estate Capital Institute.)

HOMAN SQUARE COMMUNITY CENTER AERIAL VIEW, 2005. As seen from the observation deck of the original Sears Tower, the community and surrounding newer building stretching outward give an idea as to the immense Merchandise Building that once occupied these grounds. (Courtesy of the Real Estate Capital Institute.)

Three

GREAT ARTIFACTS

*Extensive use of merchandise branding to establish quality and product differentiation is
a hallmark of Sears' success as one of the greatest retailers in America.
Allstate and Sears Tower are two examples of strong product
recognition spanning more than seven decades.*
—Myron Lyskanycz, partner in Ideasphere and
former managing director of Leo Burnett

Sears was very proud of its catalog complex, developing product names and ideas that identified with this property. A few of those names and marketing concepts developed at the plant still exist and are widely used even today.

The plant was not only a state-of-the-art manufacturing and distribution facility, but a way for Sears to effectively market itself based on the property dynamics. Brand names associated with the store were physical proof of the complex's importance beyond simply the fact of being a corporate headquarters.

So powerful was the plant's influence that the company chose to preserve the complex after moving in 1974 to the then tallest building in the world: the Sears Tower. The company also honored the location by branding select merchandise sold with names referring to the site. Many of the items become household names, including *Homart* (Homan Avenue and Arthington Street), *Tower* (original Sears Tower as part of the Merchandise Building) and *Allstate* (automotive brand that later became one of the nation's largest insurance companies). A small sampling of these marketing and sales artifacts is shown throughout this chapter.

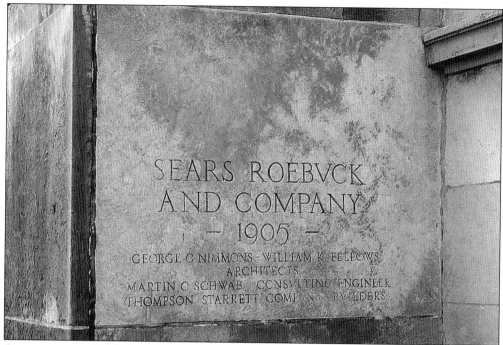

CORNERSTONE, 1906. Sears chose the base of the Tower as the cornerstone of the plant. The Tower still stands as a beacon of Sears's success and the gateway to the city's West Side. Although the cornerstone states 1905 as the year of completion, the complex officially opened in January 1906. (Courtesy of the Real Estate Capital Institute.)

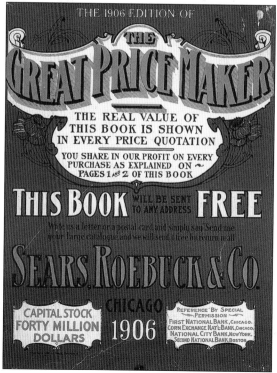

SEARS CATALOG COVER PAGE, 1906. Seen here is the first catalog issued by the plant operations. (Courtesy of Real Estate Capital Institute.)

AUTOMATIC PHONE ADVERTISEMENT, 1914. The Automatic Phone Company promoted the complex as one of the most important users of the system and a technically advanced facility of the era. (Courtesy of the Real Estate Capital Institute.)

WLS Radio Announcement, 1925. A radio bulletin proudly displays the facilities as part of its advertising. (Courtesy of WLS Radio, ABC Broadcasting Company of Chicago.)

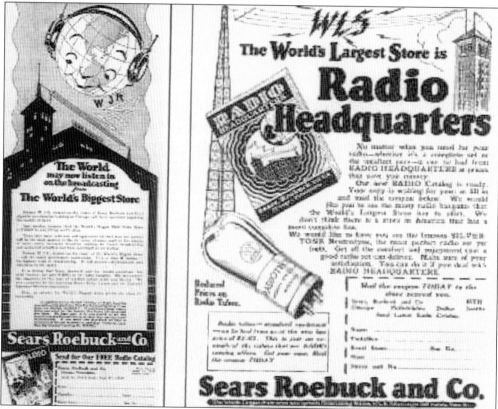

WLS Radio Advertisement, 1925. Shown here is a typical Sears radio advertisement. It refers to WLS as "World's Largest Store." (Courtesy of WLS Radio, ABC Broadcasting Company of Chicago.)

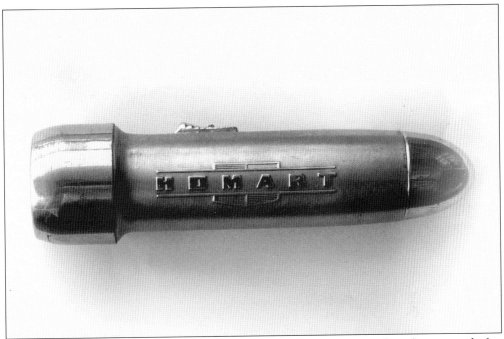

HOMART FLASHLIGHT, 1934. Homeowners throughout America owned products named after the main intersection of the complex. (Courtesy of the Real Estate Capital Institute.)

TOWER TYPEWRITER, 1950. Well before the construction of the current Sears Tower in 1973, consumers associated the original Sears Tower with the company's products. (Courtesy of the Real Estate Capital Institute.)

MERCHANDISE BUILDING BRICK, 1994. This souvenir brick commemorates the Merchandise Building and its life span. The dismantlement of this structure was advertised as one of the largest such assignments of the time. (Courtesy of the Homan Arthington Foundation.)

TOWER LOGO, 1950. Various measuring equipment bore this logo, seen here in a close-up. (Courtesy of the Real Estate Capital Institute.)

PROMOTIONAL ITEMS, 1920s. A return mailing envelope and a merchandise tag provides advertising space for Sears. (Courtesy of the Real Estate Capital Institute.)

PARKING LOT, C. 1960. Bold signs are visible in this view. (Courtesy of the Chicago Historical Society.)

OCEANS 12 MOVIE, 2004. George Clooney and Matt Damon along with a host of other celebrities filmed a scene in the Power House for this blockbuster. (Courtesy of Zreview Web site.)

STRANGER THAN FICTION, 2005. For this movie, Emma Thompson (right) filmed a night scene in front of the Tower. The author's daughter appears near the Tower with the renowned British actress. (Courtesy of the Real Estate Capital Institute.)

Four

GREAT PEOPLE

A great community must include decisive and committed leadership
creating infrastructure for the purpose of helping people to help themselves.
—Charles H. Shaw, chairman of the Shaw Company

Most important of all are the people who built, promoted, and ultimately saved the complex for generations to marvel and enjoy. Describing the time and energy dedicated into acquiring, designing, developing, operating, upgrading, and adaptively reusing the complex can easily require writing another book on this subject. And the story can be as colorful and interesting as the bricks and mortar of the facilities themselves.

This chapter covers but a small fraction of the individuals who made the catalog plant the "greatest" and its builders "great people." Many of those responsible for the complex's success over the years are also nationally renowned, including Richard Sears, Mayor Richard M. Daley, Ed Brennan, Charlie Shaw, and Charley Moran.

For nearly 100 years, North Lawndale and the property around Homan and Arthington have played prominently in people's dreams. Immigrants imagined a prosperous home in a new land. The children of the Southern migration wished for real freedom and well-paying jobs. Rosenwald, Sears, and Wood dreamed of a retailing empire. Brennan and Shaw imagined returning a historic relic to a new, useful life. And current residents dream about the full economic, social, and cultural development of their entire community.

RICHARD SEARS STEREOGRAPH, 1906. Sears sits at his desk at the complex. (Courtesy of the Real Estate Capital Institute.)

JULIUS ROSENWALD, C. 1927. In addition to entertaining visitors, including John Rockefeller and the Prince of Sweden, Rosenwald organized Sears into a tremendously successful organization. His philanthropic pursuits included the University of Chicago, Southern Schools for African Americans, and the Museum of Science and Industry. Without a doubt, he was one of the most influential Chicagoans of the early 20th century. (Courtesy of the Chicago Historical Society.)

ROBERT WOOD, C. 1927. Rosenwald's replacement, General Wood (left) propelled Sears into a global retailing force and one of the largest companies by the 1950s. He is shown here with Julius Rosenwald celebrating the 10-millionth Allstate tire sold. (Courtesy of the Sears Archives Web site.)

EDWARD BRENNAN, 2005. A West Side native and employee of the complex during his earlier years at Sears, Brennan is credited with saving the complex while serving as chairman of Sears. Brennan understood the image and strategic value of the facilities to Sears and the surrounding community. (Courtesy of Edward Brennan.)

CHARLEY MORAN, 2002. Moran is pictured second from the left, wearing a cap, with investment executives and Charlie Shaw (second from the right). A senior Sears executive, Moran was directly responsible for working with the redevelopment team (the Shaw Company) via the Homan Arthington Foundation, which was set up to preserve and enhance the value of the complex. In addition to his responsibilities with the foundation, Moran served as chairman of the Denny's Restaurant chain. He was credited with many achievements while working in the complex, including the construction of a series of skywalks between buildings to improve traffic flow. (Courtesy of the Homan Arthington Foundation.)

RICHARD M. DALEY, 2002. Chicago's mayor since 1988, Daley is one of the most proactive officials in the nation and was recently ranked as one of the top five mayors as well. He continues his father's policy of urban redevelopment on a citywide scale, wholeheartedly supporting the Homan Square project from its inception. Daley is shown here at the Community Center ribbon cutting in 2001. (Courtesy of the Homan Arthington Foundation.)

CHARLES H. SHAW, 2005. This world-renowned developer originally moved to Chicago from New York in the mid-1960s. Famous Chicago projects developed by Shaw include Lake Point Tower, the Chicago Hilton and Towers (former Stevens Hotel) renovation, and Garibaldi Square. Shaw was chosen by Sears chairman Ed Brennan and senior vice-president Charley Moran in 1988 to redevelop the catalog plant. He successfully redeveloped much of the complex into Homan Square. (Courtesy of the Real Estate Capital Institute.)

ALDERMAN MICHAEL CHANDLER, 2005. Since taking office in 1995, Chandler has proven to be a champion local civic leader, pushing for the continued improvement of North Lawndale, with the complex being one of the area's main anchors. (Courtesy of the Real Estate Capital Institute.)

CONGRESSMAN DANNY K. DAVIS, 2005. Taking office in 1996, West Side resident Davis represents the Seventh Congressional District, which includes much of the central part of the city and the West Side. He is a strong proponent of bringing investment and jobs to economically impacted communities such as the Catalog District. Davis gives federal recognition to the area by calling the Administration Building his home office. (Courtesy of the Real Estate Capital Institute.)

Five

GREAT LOCATION

*The area now known as Homan Square, which for many years anchored the
Sears Roebuck merchandising empire, contains tremendous history. It fell upon
hard times as urban changes took place. Fortunately, it is now on a serious track of
redevelopment and is one of the most exciting neighborhoods in metropolitan Chicagoland.*
—Congressman Danny K. Davis, Seventh Congressional District

*North Lawndale is truly a hidden gem. One of Chicago's
great neighborhoods is being rediscovered.*
—Alderman Michael Chandler, 25th Ward

At the dawn of the 20th century, Chicago was one of the most rapidly growing cities in the world. The population had increased from around 300,000 at the time of the Great Fire of 1871 to 1.7 million by 1900. The city was a juggernaut of economic growth and the industrial hub of the nation. The phenomenally successful 1893 World's Fair put the city at the center of the international stage.

Chicago's incredible growth came at a price, however. Social unrest reached epic proportions, culminating with the 1886 Haymarket Riots and Pullman Strikes. Against this backdrop, Sears and Rosenwald plotted the foundations of their empire. In planning their new retail merchandising headquarters, they needed to balance business efficiencies, corporate profits, and manufacturing logistics with safe and clean working conditions.

To accomplish their vision, Sears's executives had to find a location that satisfied the needs of customers, suppliers, and the workforce. Lawndale, in the heart of Chicago's West Side and just 15 minutes from Chicago's business district, was the perfect site. The 55-acre parcel encircling Homan Avenue and Arthington Street had access to critical transportation infrastructure, space for additional buildings, and accessibility for employees. Closing a street created a contiguous 1,250-by-340-foot lot, a space suitable for the new Sears Merchandise Building, the largest wood-frame building in the world.

Upon completion in 1906, the facility operated continuously until Sears moved its headquarters to the newly constructed Sears Tower at Wacker and Franklin in 1973. The merchandising facility remained in use until it was disassembled in 1994 to make way for the Homan Square redevelopment. Conditions in the neighborhood created by past economic, social, and political upheaval were not taken as problems, but rather opportunities for creating a new model of an urban community. Today, Homan and Arthington is once again a location for bold plans.

WEST SIDE PARK, 1906. The Chicago Cubs played here, about a mile and a half directly east of the Catalog Plant, and won two World Series (1907 and 1908) prior to relocating to Wrigley Field in 1914. (Courtesy of the Chicago Historical Society.)

MODEL J

SEARS AUTOMOBILE CATALOG, 1910. The company was very proud of its West Side roots, featuring the Garfield park bandshell as a background in the brochures. (Courtesy of the Real Estate Capital Institute.)

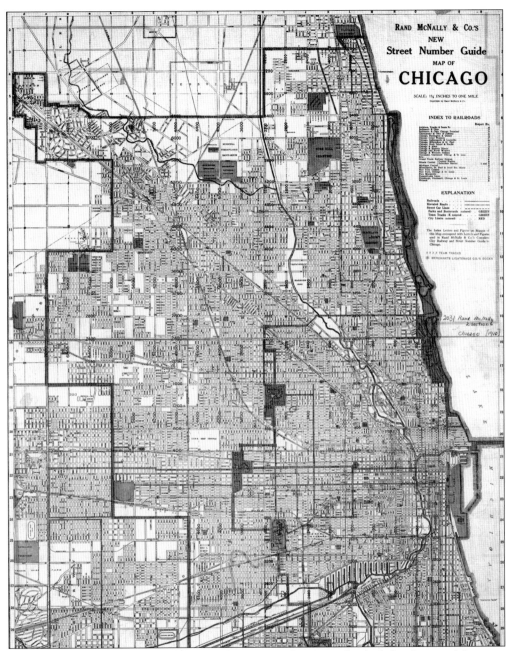

CHICAGO MAP, 1900. A century ago, the Chicago Park System clearly defined some of the more prominent communities in the city. Note the vacant block of land soon to be the new Sears headquarters. (Courtesy of the Real Estate Capital Institute.)

DOUGLAS PARK PAVILION, 1905. Established in 1869 and named after the great Illinois politician famous for debating Abraham Lincoln, Douglas Park is one of Chicago's oldest and most beautiful. It is located a quarter-mile southeast of the catalog plant. (Courtesy of the Real Estate Capital Institute.)

DOUGLAS PARK BATH HOUSE, 1905. Public and private bathhouses were popular a century ago, as few homes had the staple of today's bathroom: the bathtub. These spots were also popular as summer retreats from heat and humidity. The "I Will" logo on the postcard is Chicago's motto, with the letter "Y" showing the Chicago River branching out. (Courtesy of the Real Estate Capital Institute.)

GARFIELD PARK PAVILION, 1905. Also established in 1869 and originally known as Central Park (for designer Fredrick Law Olmsted, creator of New York's Central Park), this space was renamed after President Garfield in the late 1880s. The park, a half-mile north of the complex, is famous for its conservatory, field house, and various pavilions. (Courtesy of the Real Estate Capital Institute.)

DOUGLAS PARK AUDITORIUM, 1915. This famous commercial landmark is located a half-mile south of the complex. During the auditorium's heyday prior to World War II, many performers trained here, including Tony Curtis. (Courtesy of the Real Estate Capital Institute.)

DOUGLAS PARK PAVILION, 1920. This image provides another view of one of Douglas Park's treasures. The park is a half-mile south of the complex. (Courtesy of the Real Estate Capital Institute.)

GARFIELD PARK LILY POND, 1925. The lily ponds attracted locals and Chicago visitors alike to this park, only a 10-minute train ride from downtown. (Courtesy of the Real Estate Capital Institute.)

GARFIELD PARK AERIAL VIEW, 1930. This postcard describes the hotel on the west side of Garfield Park as a convenient location with excellent transportation linkages. Today, the train line pictured at left is the Eisenhower Expressway (Interstate 290). (Courtesy of the Real Estate Capital Institute.)

GARFIELD PARK AERIAL, 2002. Shown here is a recent northward view of the park. (Courtesy of the Real Estate Capital Institute.)

GARFIELD PARK CONSERVATORY, 2002. One of the largest in the nation, this two-acre conservatory was built in 1907 and extensively remodeled during the past couple of years. During 2002, the conservatory hosted the Chihuly glass sculpture exhibit, attracting more than 800,000 visitors. (Courtesy of the Real Estate Capital Institute.)

DOUGLAS PARK BOULEVARD SIGN, 2002. Outside of Chicago's central business district (the Loop), the most architecturally significant landmark is the park district's extensive system of boulevards, otherwise known as the "Emerald Necklace." The extensively landscaped boulevards link Chicago's main parks of Douglas, Garfield, Humboldt, Washington, Jackson, and Lincoln. The complex abuts Independence Boulevard, which connects Douglas and Garfield Parks. (Courtesy of the Real Estate Capital Institute.)

Typical Historic Housing on the West Side, 2004. The West Side is rich in architectural treasures like Wicker Park, Tri-Taylor, Pilsen, Garfield Park, the Ukrainian Village, and North Lawndale. Most notably beautiful, vintage greystone two-flats are found throughout this area. (Courtesy of the Real Estate Capital Institute.)

Original Sears Tower and Chicago Skyline, 2004. Also known as the first Sears Tower, this 14-story structure stands as the beacon of North Lawndale. The Tower is the oldest skyscraper in the city outside of the downtown area. Along with the nearby Sears Administration and Printing Buildings, it is a federal and city landmark protected by the U.S. Park Service. (Courtesy of the Real Estate Capital Institute.)

COMPLEX IN 1914 (ABOVE) AND TODAY (2005). The view looking southwest at the Administration Building and Tower remains almost identical with the exception of the removal of the Tower-attached Merchandise Building. (Courtesy of the Real Estate Capital Institute.)

FALCON, 2005. A set of federally and locally protected Peregrine falcons are a tourist attraction. These birds make the Tower and Power House chimney their home. More importantly, these majestic birds come to represent the free spirit and energy of all who have made the area great. (Courtesy of the Real Estate Capital Institute.)

ORIGINAL SEARS TOWER AND CURRENT SEARS TOWER, 2005. This photograph, taken from Independence Boulevard, shows the two towers lining up to form the "Sears Twins." (Courtesy of the Real Estate Capital Institute.)